Revival, Toronto and the Church Today

William J. Abraham
William R. Davies
G. Howard Mellor

CLIFF COLLEGE PUBLISHING
CALVER, SHEFFIELD S30 1XG Tel: BASLOW (01246) 582321

ISBN 1 898362 13 0
© 1995 Cliff College Publishing

All rights reserved. No part of this publication may be reproduced, stored in a retrieval system, or transmitted in any form or by any means, electronic, mechanical, photocopying, recording or otherwise, without the prior written permission of the publisher.

Cliff College Publishing, Calver, Sheffield S30 1XG

Printed by

MOORLEY'S Print & Publishing
23 Park Rd., Ilkeston, Derbys DE7 5DA
Tel/Fax: (0115) 932 0643

from data supplied on disk

Awakening in Toronto 1994:
Personal Report and Reflections
William J. Abraham
Perkins School of Theology, Southern Methodist University

In what follows I want to provide a bare-bones account of my visit to Toronto which lasted from Thursday 25 August until Thursday 1 September, 1994. I had heard of there being a significant spiritual awakening through a former student who had visited several weeks before and through an article in Newsweek in early or middle August. I have studied the history of revival for years, and yearly teach a course on the relation between revivalism and evangelism. I have been following developments in renewal circles now for over ten years.[1]

I

The awakening began on January 20, 1994 in the Toronto Airport Vineyard.[2] On that occasion an individual present, claiming to speak in the name of the demonic, challenged the church during a time of prophecy by demanding to know if they had a God who had a word for him. This led to a deep encounter with God in the meeting. Out of this evening meetings began. It has continued every night, except Mondays when there are no evening meetings. There were in the region of 600-700 people present each of the nights that I was there. The place is absolutely packed to capacity.

The Vineyard here is pretty much the standard type, modeled and supervised by John Wimber through the local leaders. It is an absolutely unprepossessing building, more like a warehouse than anything else. It is located on Dixie Road, in the corner of a kind of shopping center, next door to a Post Office, a building the leaders would dearly love to take over due to the crowding. Basically all there is inside is a stage for the worship leaders, with floor-space filled with chairs which can be lifted up and folded to the side when necessary. From time to time one can hear the faint echo of jet aircraft taking off from the airport. Next door there is a cornfield.

II

I arrived here on Thursday and reached the building for the evening service at 7.30 p.m. The place was already packed to capacity; an overflow room was also full. I found a place at the back, next to a wall so that I could have a place to lean. There was an extraordinary diversity of people: young, old, middle-aged, children; representatives from many major groups in the world: England, Ireland, Wales, Scotland, Norway, Belgium, Austria, France, Germany, South Africa, Nicaragua, India,

Argentina, Zimbabwe, Hong Kong, Nigeria, North America, Canada. During the week one lost count of the countries represented. Some had come from abroad at very little notice; they heard word of the events in Toronto and took a day or two to prepare and come. The atmosphere was noisy, slightly tense, expectant, casual.

The next day I showed up at 7.00 p.m. hoping to get a seat. I found myself at the back of a long line; when I got in all the seats were gone. On the following day I got there two hours early, and waited in line for over an hour and a half to ensure that I got a seat. This was the situation night after night. The people waiting were patient, quiet, and resilient.

Each evening during the first week they changed the band and worship leaders. The style of music was decidedly contemporary, at times approaching very, very soft rock. The musicianship was of very high technical quality. The current leaders of the church were not there the first week, as they are away at an annual church camp north of here. The main leader was a pastor from a Vineyard church about one hundred miles north of New York. He had been a very conservative Baptist, an executive with IBM, and a thoroughgoing dispensationalist before meeting John Wimber and the Vineyard movement in 1985. He was a little out of his depth at times - something he himself knew - and his fundamentalist background would come through in a kind of inverted way at times, as when he would have a sideswipe at his fundamentalist past. He overreached in his sermon on Sunday night; he is still working through what it is like to speak to large crowds. He had a lovely spirit and the core commitments were very clear and solid. The fundamental issue was God's love for his people and for the world. This comes through again and again. Hence the physical manifestation they regularly witnessed were not the heart of the work of God but inexplicable events which were to be judged by historical precedent in the life of the church, by potential biblical patterns, and by moral and spiritual fruit. The associate pastor led worship on Saturday night. He had a very conservative background (a graduate of Grace Seminary); he had been a school principal for 12 years; he spoke very little but when he did, he was a very gifted speaker with brilliant turn of phrase and a very expressive face.

The senior pastor, John Arnott, spoke on Sunday morning and on the other evenings. He came across as a very, very fine leader. One sensed that he had known suffering, that he had absolutely no personal stake in what was going on, that he was genuinely humble, that he had bags of pastoral experience working with real people, and that he had no axes to grind. During the ministry time as the evening wore on, it was clear that he was very tired. On Sunday he preached on Ephesians 4, providing a fine exposition in a disarming manner, without any rhetorical tricks. He has a deep compassion for people and a passion to let God work sovereignty. He is a natural leader who shows no interest in his own reputation or standing.

III

The services follow a simple pattern.

1. There is almost one hour of worship, singing the standard type Vineyard hymns, repeating them several times over. Sometimes there is shift from rousing material at the beginning to much softer material at the end. The leader will sometimes lead in very short prayers of adoration and invocation. On Friday night the spirit of the meeting was positively festive. Once or twice there was a communal singing in tongues, although many sang in English during this time. On one occasion there was a message in tongues; this was followed by an interpretation by a woman from Ireland. The message was one of intense longing on the part of God to love and bless his people.

2. Those who were there for the first time were asked to raise their hands. Participants from different parts of the world identified themselves and were greeted with applause. There is a sense among the people that God is using the meetings in Toronto on a wider scale. Not a penny has been spent on publicity or advertising. The international, multicultural character of the meetings is very striking.

3. There is about a half hour of testimony. The speaker had already picked out three or four people to interview, asking them what was happening, how they had come, what they were experiencing, and the like. There was great stress on the need to let God be sovereign in what He did and on the core issue being the believer's relationship with God. Physical manifestations were totally relativized and played down. Clearly a concerted effort is being made to provide some kind of focus for the meetings, while at the same time being open to whatever God may want to do. At the end of the interview, there is special ministry for the person interviewed. In virtually every case they fell to the ground, many of them lying there for an hour thereafter. There was great honesty during the interviews, with no attempt to prove a point other than to keep stressing that the real issue was love for God, the coming of the kingdom, and owning personal responsibility for service empowered by the Holy Spirit.

4. There is an offering. There was no hype for money. Mention was made of the need to move to bigger facilities and nothing else. At times they seem to have forgotten to organize ushers.

5. There is about a forty minute sermon. This is simple in structure and content, taking the form of a rambling, earthy interpretation of a passage of scripture related to the theme of the coming of the Kingdom of God or the great love of God for his people, interspersed with comment and story. The sermons end with a brief evangelistic appeal; in most cases there was a small response. Clearly nearly all present were already Christians.

6. After the sermon the worship team took over again. No outsiders or visitors were allowed to be part of the prayer and ministry team. The team members were identified by simple name stickers which disclosed that they were on the team for the evening. On the first week the team were mostly from the Vineyard from New York. The chairs were stacked and placed alongside the wall. The ministry team started at the front and worked their way to the back.

The atmosphere throughout remained totally calm, even casual. For individuals the situation was often totally different. Scores ended up on the floor and would lie there for up to and well beyond a half an hour. I walked across the room to go to the restroom and had to pick my way carefully through the bodies all over the floor. During the worship one or two developed uncontrollable shaking; this recurred in their case during the time of ministry. A few roared in agony, bending over, as if they were working through some terrible grief. One or two had uncontrollable jerking, bouncing up and down for half an hour. Some fell without any special ministry at all. This was dangerous because usually there were people assigned to catch those about to fall, but nobody got hurt and those standing close by quickly caught on to be on the lookout. Some people laughed uncontrollably on the floor for twenty minutes and more.

It was clear that many individuals were going through very critical encounters with God. This came out in the testimonies. There were a significant number of pastors present, although these were not singled out for special attention. In the seven months between five and six thousand pastors have come through. One pastor from South Africa, seminary trained, clearly had the encounter of his life. It involved many elements: a fresh call to ministry and discipleship, a vision of the sins of his church and nation, an unspeakable sense of God's love and peace. A pastor from Wales told of a Rev. Griffiths who had been in the Welsh Revival of 1906 and had passed on what had happened then. He had prayed that the young men in the ministry would live to see what he had seen; this had now happened, complete with a vision of angels in the sky over the airport, taking the power of God to the four corners of the earth. The vision took place in his hotel room. In every case the individual was simply left alone after ministry to soak in the presence of God and work through their particular encounter with the Holy Spirit.

One remarkable encounter involved a young pastor from Belfast. He had been the kind of person who could not stand any kind of interruption in a church service; everything had to be tightly controlled from start to finish. His life has been totally turned upside down at the church camp meetings. He fell into uncontrollable laughter for forty minutes, then took to a kind of surfing. In the Tuesday evening service he was in a kind of drunken stupor, unable to talk properly during the interview but obviously filled with deep joy. He had obviously been liberated and set free from a rigid, inflexible piety.

One evening one young man ended up on all fours, crawling and growling like a lion from one end of the building to another. Nobody was bothered by it. It was taken as almost a natural occurrence, between the individual and God, signifying the Lion of Judah's power and strength. Most people were too caught up in their waiting on God to pay attention.

People began to drift away from about 11.00 p.m. I left usually before midnight. The services did not finish until 2.00 to 2.30 a.m. People were very relaxed, standing around, leaning up against the chairs around the walls.

7. From about 10.00 p.m. there is a skeleton cafe open; there is also a small bookstore with books and tapes.

IV

On Mondays and Thursdays there is a prayer meeting from 1.30 until 3.30 p.m. On the Monday, when I attended, there were about thirty people, with a strong sprinkling of people from England. One was a lecturer in church history from the Bristol area. There were three women beside me who had traveled five hours to get there and were staying until Friday. One of the women was from a small town not far from where I was born in Ireland. The leader was a woman who was exceptionally strong and sensitive as a leader. The format was simple and very effective.

1. A time of quiet personal confession before God.

2. A time of waiting and listening before God. Individuals recorded on paper various biblical verses, word pictures, visions.

3. These were shared with the groups as a whole. Two of the visions were very vivid pictures, one of a feast made available by Christ for his people, another of the sorry state of the church as a whole. A set of common themes gradually emerged. Today the theme was the need to listen carefully to God and not to do God's work in merely human strength and wisdom.

4. Intercession followed for about an hour related to the material which had earlier been shared with the group.

The time went by remarkably quickly. The atmosphere was almost businesslike. A couple of individuals shook or twitched in their hands and arms. There was a total lack of official piety. When it was over, people stood around in small groups for a while and then dispersed.

V

On Wednesdays at noon there is a meeting for pastors. This begins with light lunch and coffee. There is obviously a great compassion for pastors here. There were over two hundred a fifty there, including spouses. The meeting itself began at 12.30 and the ministry time was still going strong when I left before 5.00.

After twenty minutes of worship, there was an excellent address by Dr. Guy Chevreau on some of the features of earlier revivals. Material was draw from Hilary of Poitiers, John Wesley, and Howell Harris. The focus, however, was on Jonathan Edwards. Particular attention was given to the experiences of his wife. Several here have undergone similar extended periods of intense immersion in the Holy Spirit. Clearly Edwards has become a significant figure in the efforts to interpret what has been happening. There is substantial material on Edwards in the bookstore. Chevreau has a Th.D. from St. Michael's in Toronto in the theology and history of spirituality. He has been a Baptist pastor. His talk was quiet, substantial, and carefully measured. After he spoke there were shorter talks by John Arnott, the senior pastor, and Mark Dupont, an associate pastor. There was a short time for questions, most of which focused on very practical questions about various aspects of ministry in the Toronto context. A delegation of African Americans were keen to find out how far the were reaching the African American community. The youth pastor here is an African American who suggested that there were significant cultural factors related to the level of impact. I personally was struck by the extensive inclusivism of the crowds who have come.

After the various talks, there was an extended period of ministry in the overflow room. Within half an hour the floor was littered with bodies. A few lay speaking in tongues; some were quietly laughing and chuckling; some were moaning, as if in agony. About a quarter stood quietly before the Lord in prayer. The meeting was led by Mark Dupont in a quiet, efficient manner, helped out by a predesignated ministry team.

VI

My own impressions of the meetings as a whole are as follows.

1. There is here clearly a recurrence of the phenomena which have occurred regularly in earlier awakenings in Europe and North America. The physical manifestations are very similar, if not identical. The prayer often heard from the ministry team "More, Lord, More!" was often used in the Welsh revival of 1906.

2. The leaders here are clearly aware of the historical precedents, even though their historical knowledge is probably scanty and confined to a few. A book by one of the leaders is currently at press and will be out in October.[3] Jonathan Edwards is the most frequently mentioned name from history. John Wesley is a close second. Yet there is no desire to emulate the past or to see this as a recurrence of earlier awakenings.

3. Word is clearly getting out, people are showing up from everywhere, and when they go back, they are seeing similar meetings and phenomena in their home situations. Two hundred pastors are meeting in London, England. The secular press have picked up the story and so far have not been negative. There has been a short clip on the Television news.

4. There is a distinctive ethos here. The dress is very casual; the music is upbeat; the theology stresses the coming of the Kingdom, the presence of the Spirit, the extraordinary love and mercy of God for all. There is an undercurrent of opposition to formal religion and to Pharaisaism within the church, yet there is a great love for the church and sincere distress over its failures and sin.

5. Behind and underneath the scenes, there are solid and very shrewd leaders who are constantly processing what is going on, but who are reluctant or opposed to organizing what is happening. There is a kind of holy fear of quenching the Spirit. A conference is planned for October 12-15. They have already worked through the basic institutional structures which are thus far most useful. Clearly extended meetings and conferences are very fundamental.

6. There is a very impressive body of lay people involved in the ministry to individual persons. There is no manipulation. The people who take part in the ministry time are veterans; they have been at this for a long time. Others are yoked with veterans in training.

7. There is a deep spirit of unity and a strong opposition to sectarianism and any kind of denominationalism.

8. The leaders strike me as coming from conservative backgrounds who have had very fixed theologies which have had to be abandoned in the wake of the manifestations of the power of God. There is at times a note of anti-intellectualism and a distaste for analysis, but this is not obtrusive. Yet the leaders themselves know that they cannot avoid exploring what all these happenings means, and they are clearly working on the theological significance as best they can. There all sorts of implicit theological convictions at work in describing what is happening. They have their own scholars working quietly behind the scenes.

9. Young people are significantly involved. Two girls in their early teens were trainee team members. The effects of their ministry were little different from that of adults. Children and young people have been receiving and responding pretty much like the adults.

10. There are a few odd-balls present, but many, many less than one might expect. One man struck me as keen to manufacture his own encounter with God; two women were clearly there for a kind of physical and spiritual roller-coaster; in another case the shaking struck me as self-induced and self-perpetuated. One woman, from India, engaged in a beautiful form of dancing before God, one evening at the back and another evening at the front. The same happened with another woman from India on two other evenings. I sensed a lot of pain in some faces; many of those who had come struck me as being burnt out and beaten. Many others were very relaxed and quietly open to whatever God might do.

Some were probably disappointed that nothing happened to them, but so much happened to so many that it would be hard to say how far this mattered overall. Those not personally blessed were blessed seeing others being deeply touched by God.

VII

Why have people come to these meetings?

People clearly have come here because they are hungry and because their churches have failed them in various ways. One man I met from Seattle had a Roman Catholic background. He is well educated, a contractor, now helping as a lay associate pastor in a small church. While on drugs he had an encounter with the demonic in the form of a spirit of fear, suicide, and destruction, and his church had absolutely nothing to offer him to get through this. He has wandered all over the religious map and is now developing a keen interest in his Roman Catholic background and theology. He came because he needed a break; his wife had packed him off to be refreshed.

A young woman from Mexico whose father is a Pentecostal pastor comes because her own church has become rather fixed and closed. She does not yet know what to do with the fact that the senior pastor has been divorced. Another young man from Mexico is shopping for a church home and was confused about the phenomena yet hopeful that something dramatic might happen to him. Another man from England, who had been transferred with his family from London by IBM, had come to the Vineyard as his home church with this family. He will probably be in Toronto for three years and sees this as a great bonus.

VIII

How does this compare with other awakenings?

1. The similarities with early awakenings are in the region of the following: a deep sense of worship; a sense of the presence of God in the meetings; various physical manifestations; a recovery of core elements of the faith; no interest in sticking to a prearranged schedule; intercession; music that fits the style and experience of the participants; uncertainty about what all this means; intense personal encounter with God, involving repentance, peace, assurance, and love; concern for the lost and needy; distrust of or unease with intellectual analysis, yet intense curiosity and a strong desire to have some sort of theological explanation for what is happening; a yearning for unity among Christians.

2. The dissimilarities are probably along these lines: the physical manifestations are taken as clear signs of God's power and presence; various gifts of the Spirit [prophecy, healing] are taken as natural givens; extremely strong emphasis on lay ministry; wariness about providing organizational structures or a fixed theological analysis; no big-name leaders.

3. Clearly what is happening here has been going on for some time among various groups in the Third world. It will be very interesting to see

a) if this continues to spread elsewhere, and
b) if Toronto becomes the symbol and icon of a wider movement.

The BBC sent a full team over to cover the awakening after similar phenomena broke out in London. My own judgment is that collectively what is happening is a kind of Awakening. The difficulty in making this kind of judgment is that Awakenings are really a kind of historical construct which can only be applied retrospectively. They are much more diffuse than appears in the narratives which describe them afterwards. They are really a loose network of happenings which are seen as part of a wider pattern later.[4] Outsiders and insiders have radically different perspectives on them.

IX

What is the possible significance of these meetings?

The current widespread happenings reflect a host of complex factors. Chief among them are:

1. The hunger in the modern world for intense religious experience and encounter with God has fostered radical forms of experiments to find food within the framework of the Christian tradition. There is a radical dissatisfaction with the boredom of the modern church and a readiness to enter something significantly different from anything which has happened in the past.

2. The failure of the modern church to meet the emotional needs of people in worship and to deal with the kind of radical evil which many are wrestling with underneath the surface is being compensated for here by very effective forms of ministry. It is quite impossible to distinguish between clergy and laity; all engage in some form of ministry.

3. The inadequacy of all forms of modern theology, both conservative, liberal, and radical to mediate the transcendent mystery, power, and presence of God, most especially the dynamic, supernatural aspects of the Holy Spirit is reflected in the attraction of these meetings to a wide cross-section of modern Christians.

4. This kind of worship and style of spirituality is clearly reaching a significant segment of the current generation.

5. The old divisions and issues of the church are no longer relevant to a lot of people. It is as if Christianity is being invented from the ground up all over again.

6. One way to think about these events is to see them as simply a time of intense waiting on God using some of the classical means of grace. These meetings are intense retreats where people are serious about their relationship with God and where they undergo a deep meeting with the divine order.

7. There is a strong stress on the need for the church to be renewed, if it is to reach out to the hurting and the needy and bring them to Christ. Renewal is seen as integral to effective evangelism, a topic always close to the surface here.

X

What challenges are having to be faced?

The issues those in leadership face are the following.

1. How to inhibit personally manufactured happenings while remaining open to the sovereign working of God.

   This is not really a serious problem as there is simple structure to the services and most people would be much too afraid to play at religion, given the sense of the presence of God and the quality of the leadership here.

2. How to avoid falling into anti-intellectualism, all the while deploying all sorts of theological convictions and judgments.

   The theological work required will take generations to be worked out. The fundamental issues are clear: there is here a recovery of basic gospel materials presented with an unprofessional freshness.

3. How to answer the extensive criticism launched against them by conservatives and fundamentalists.

   The leaders take this more seriously than I suspect is warranted. Yet the criticism keeps them honest and alert.

4. How to fit what is happening into a network of events across the world and into the development and evolution of their own mostly unrecognized tradition.

   For the most part this is left dangling, as nobody really knows how these events fit in with other happenings.

5. How to find fit expression for their concern for evangelism and outreach to the poor.

   The natural tendency in evangelism is to fall back on the conventional evangelistic strategies, updated with some church growth insights; in outreach to the poor the strategy is to engage in sporadic forays with food and blankets to the homeless.[5] There is also a strong undercurrent of opposition to reliance on human strategy and planning in evangelism. The stress is on divine initiative and wisdom. Given that most present are visitors, the stress on the whole is on the need for a recovery of one's first love for God.

6. How to keep at bay the various forms of heretical and bizarre teaching on spirituality and money currently swirling around in the Protestant underworld and in those circles which gravitate to the language of revival and awakening.

   The strategy appears to stick closely to the basics of the faith and to the bible. I am sure that the thinking of John Wimber has a profound formative influence through the leaders.

7. How to relate what is happening to biblical and historical materials.

   Some of these issues are addressed in the sermons in the evening meetings.

8. How to avoid pride and judgmentalism, and how to promote true holiness.

These are also addressed in the sermons and talks. There is a recurring emphasis on the need for a deep relationship with God as a living, mysterious agent of love and change.

9. How to develop a deep theology which can accommodate suffering, mystery in the ways of God, supernatural intervention, bizarre physical phenomena, and the gifts of the Holy Spirit, and yet which will not harden into a closed form of orthodoxy.

   There is a strong tendency to avoid theological systems. The general line is to put theology on hold for the present. There is a strong antipathy to any kind of overemphasis on doctrine.

10. How to develop appropriate forms of liturgy which will express a deeper scriptural content and avoid slipping into sentimentality and overuse of romantic imagery.

    Already there is a relatively set liturgy, although few here would recognize this. One naturally thinks of Wesley's hymns as a radical alternative, but I suspect that this is now lost, or it would take extensive updating musically to fit.

11. How to help people work through the complexity of the spiritual life and the great variety of experiences which people undergo here.

    There is a very healthy emphasis on the unpredictability of what may happen and a strong stress on the progressive character of what happens in the life of an individual. The latter comes out very strongly in the testimonies. There is a strong desire to get away from an easy, quick-fix spirituality, even though many people have dramatic encounters and experiences which are life-changing.

12. How to develop ecclesial structures to contain the energy which is let loose on occasions like this.

    For the most part this is ignored because there is a great fear of institutionalism or because those who come are already part of a church or ecclesial structure. However, awakenings invariably have an impact on the structures of the church, so this is worth watching over time.

XI

On my first night here one of the leaders described this place as a watering hole. This is a very apt description. This awakening shows the church that there are deep resources in the very being of God for the transformation of individual persons, of local congregations, of the church as a whole, and of the wider cultures of the nations. On the wider scheme of things, it would be a serious mistake to limit God's working to these kinds of meetings. Yet what is happening here is profoundly authentic; Western Christianity has been renewed again and again by these kinds of meetings. The revivalism of the nineteeth century is over and gone, but revival is alive and well in Toronto. Awakening is being reinvented all over again in the late twentieth century.

Notes:

1. Currently one can attend the Airport Vineyard in the same way one would attend any formal conference. There are special arrangements with local hotels. One of the managers is thrilled to know that there is no end in sight.

2. The Vineyard is the name adopted by local churches which have grown through the work of John Wimber who pastors a large church in Anaheim, California. Wimber was originally the manager of the Righteous Brothers in Las Vegas. After a remarkable conversion he became a pastor, a field-worker in the area of church growth, and eventually entered into a very significant spiritual journey which has led him into a worldwide ministry of renewal. With Kevin Springer, he has written two significant books related to evangelism and renewal: Power Evangelism and Power Healing, both published by Harper and Row. The airport Vineyard is a young church, about five years old. It currently has a membership of about 450 people.

3. The book is to be called "Catch the Fire".

4. I have already picked up reports from a reliable source in England that there are already mixed developments in England. Some of the meetings have attracted and been dominated by a fair number of religous nuts and cranks; others are much more authentic. This mixture of type is typical of past awakenings.

5. On Saturday and Sunday night teams went down town to bring food to the homeless. This was led by a very impressive young woman in her early twenties. Some of the stories reported back from Saturday night on Sunday were extraordinarily moving.

JOHN WESLEY, HEALING AND THE TORONTO BLESSING

Bill Davies
(Formerly Principal of Cliff College and a Past President of the Methodist Conference.)

John Wesley's great interest in healing was of a practical kind. In December of 1746 he shared with the Methodist Society in London his plan of "giving physic to the poor". Within three weeks he had treated about 300 patients. Of these, he claimed that over 200 were made "sensibly better" and 51 were "thoroughly cured". The following year he published *Primitive Physic* which eventually ran into 32 editions. Some of the remedies it contained were very primitive.

What may not generally be known is that Wesley was one of the first to experiment with electrical treatment. His journal entry for Tuesday 9 November 1756 reads: "Having procured an apparatus on purpose, I ordered several persons to be electrified, who were ill of various disorders, some of whom found an immediate, some a gradual cure."

He evidently had a high regard for the safety of such treatment, saying that while hundreds and perhaps thousands (Wesley was never very good at estimating numbers, especially his congregations) had received unspeakable good, he had not known any man, woman or child who had received any hurt thereby.

Wesley was very cautious of some types of healing which seemed to him to indicate fanaticism. For example, he was highly critical of one George Bell who, according to Joseph Cownley, one of Wesley's preachers, exceeded all others in delusion, becoming a prophet who declared himself to be immortal, making a false prediction about the end of the world.

He was evidently the ring-leader of a group of fanatics who attempted to give sight to the blind and raise the dead. Eventually Wesley had to exclude him from the Methodist Society because of the discredit brought on a genuine work of God in 1760 and 1761, when there was an extraordinary spiritual awakening in London.

Nevertheless, there were charismatic healings in the 18th-century revival. John Wesley, writing in 1784, tells of a young woman in Oldham of unblameable character, whose word he trusted, who had a remarkable experience. She said, "I had totally lost the sight of my right eye, when I dreamed one night that our Saviour appeared to me; that I fell at his feet and he laid his hand upon my right eye. Immediately I waked, and from that moment have seen as well with that eye as with the other."

John Furz, one of Wesley's preachers, was healed at the time he had an experience of the sanctifying power of the Holy Spirit. When thought to be on his death-bed, Furz cried out to God, "Lord, sanctify me now or never!" His testimony was that he felt the mighty power of God's Spirit coming into his soul as a purifying, refining fire, cleansing him from all unrighteousness. From that moment he began to recover.

When Christopher Hopper, another of the preachers, was very ill, he was told by his doctor that he was dying. He described his experience: "I fell into a sweet rest and dreamed I was dead ... and that my spirit was with Christ in a state of unspeakable happiness; but was sent back again to call a few more sinners to repentance. I then awoke, my fever was gone, and from that moment I began to recover. My strength of body soon returned, and the Lord sent me forth with a fresh commission."

Deliverance

As deliverance from demonisation forms part of the healing ministry today it is worth noting that such experiences were also present in the Methodist Revival.

William Black tells of a young man who talked unscripturally of being led by the Spirit. He sat on a bench, grinning and grinding his teeth and appeared to be under the influence of some evil spirit. Sometimes he barked like a dog, then he would rush around the room jumping, stamping and making the most dreadful noises, mingling with his shouts, blasphemy against Jesus Christ. Black wrote: "I was peculiarly helped to wrestle with the Lord, that he would either bind or cast out the evil one. I continued praying until he became as quiet as a lamb, kneeled down by me, and began to pray."

George Shadford in America visited a man who lived near Baltimore, thought to be mad or possessed with a devil. Shadford wrestled with God in prayer and preached in the house every week or fortnight for some time. Ultimately deliverance came when the young man who was bound was loosed from the chain of his sins and set at perfect liberty.

Discernment

For Wesley, the discernment of spirits was of paramount importance. He knew that without it, untold harm could be done to the work of revival. It was not only in the discerning of those who were demonised that this gift was important, but also in testing phenomena which occurred from time to time during the whole of his ministry.

Extravagances, extremism and fanaticism needed to be "discerned". While Wesley would never oppose a genuine work of God, he was acutely aware of the havoc that could be caused by things that were not of the Holy Spirit. Wesley was critical of extremism generally. Some of the extravagances which troubled Wesley are illustrated by what he found in Chapel-en-le-Frith in 1786:

"Frequently three or four, yea, ten or twelve, pray aloud together. Some of them, perhaps many scream altogether as loud as they possibly can. Some of them use improper, yea, indecent, expressions in prayer. Several drop down as dead; and are stiff as a corpse but in a while, they start up, and cry, 'Glory! Glory!' perhaps 20 times altogether. Just so do the French prophets, and very lately the Jumpers in Wales, bring the real work into contempt."

What would Wesley have made of the Toronto blessing?

I suspect he would have given the kind of response he made in 1759 after preaching at Everton. He noticed a difference in the work from his previous visit there. No long did people go down into trances, cry out, fall down, tremble or become convulsed. Instead there was a refreshing peace.

Reflecting on what used to happen, Wesley wrote: "The danger was to regard extraordinary circumstances too much, such as outcries, convulsions, visions, trances; as if these were essential to the inward work ... Perhaps the danger is to regard them too little, to condemn them altogether; to imagine they had nothing of God in them.

"Whereas the truth is: God suddenly and strongly convinced many they were lost sinners, the natural consequence whereof were sudden outcries and bodily convulsions; to strengthen and encourage them that believed, and to make his work more apparent, he favoured several of them with divine dreams, often with trances and visions; in some of these instances, after a time, nature mixed with grace; Satan likewise mimicked this work of God, in order to discredit the whole ... At first it was, doubtless, wholly from God. It is partly so at this day; and he will enable us to discern how far in every case the work is pure, and where it mixes or degenerates ..."

While there is little evidence to suggest that Wesley practised the gift of healing in the modern charismatic sense, he certainly believed God healed in miraculous ways. This should be an encouragement to all whom God uses through prayer and the gifts of healing.

Prayer alone, prayer with the laying-on of hands, and prayer and the anointing with oil, all would find favour with Wesley, who looked to Scripture for his authority. Wesley's practice of seeking healing from natural resources should confirm us in our belief that God cannot be limited in the way he heals.

The one who advises people to throw away their tablets, trusting in faith and prayer alone, limits God, just as surely as the one who denies the gifts of healing. The importance Wesley placed upon discernment is also important for us in these days. Although there are many areas in which discernment is necessary, there are two to which attention may be drawn.

One is the ministry of deliverance itself. Although there is no evidence that Wesley engaged in exorcisms, he knew of the power of sin and the need for its power to be broken. His whole ministry was spent in attacking what today many would call the strongholds of Satan.

Among his preachers men like William Black, John Walton, George Shadford and John Nelson set people free in the name of Jesus from the demonic chains which bound them. They also realised the need for discernment.

When John Nelson was approached by a man who said that he was concerned about the state of his soul, Nelson said, "As he was coming, it was impressed upon my mind that he was a deceiver," and he told the man that Satan had sent him with a lie in his mouth.

The man started to go away but fell and "roared like a bear". He eventually asked Nelson to pray for him, which he did, but before ever Nelson began to minister, there was first that discernment, which is as necessary in ministry now as it was then.

Toronto blessing

The reference to "roaring like a bear" and other phenomena manifested in the Methodist Revival sounds like the Toronto blessing.

Falling down ("resting in the Spirit", or "being slain in the Spirit"), trembling and even roaring happened in the 18th century. These have been referred to already. There was also laughter, but Wesley did not think it to be of the Holy Spirit, at least, not in the instances recorded. Near to Bristol on 9 May 1740, Wesley was "a little surprised at some who were buffeted of Satan in an unusual manner, by a spirit of laughter as they could in no wise resist".

He recalled that the same thing had happened to himself and his brother, Charles, 10 or 11 years previously. They were walking in a meadow singing psalms when suddenly Charles burst out into loud laughter. John was angry, but then suddenly found himself laughing, too. "Nor could we possibly refrain, though we were ready to tear ourselves in pieces, but we were forced to go home without singing another line."

Another instance is described for 21 May 1740: "In the evening such a spirit of laughter was among us that many were offended." One Lucretia Smith was "so violently and variously torn of the Evil One ... sometimes she laughed ... then broke out into cursing and blaspheming ... then stamped and struggled with incredible strength ... At last she faintly called on Christ to help her, and the violence of her pangs ceased." In the same entry of his Journal, Wesley refers to Elizabeth Brown and Anne Holton who laughed for two days "and were then, upon prayer made for them, delivered in a moment".

In these instances, Wesley thought the laughter to be of the devil, even though on one occasion he was himself involved. Nowhere, however, does he say that laughter in worship or personal experience is always of the devil; the same discernment of what inspires the laughter as to what inspires other manifestations need to be applied.

It was the distracting, hysterical, uncontrollable laughter which troubled Wesley. On one occasion, having listened to a French prophetess, Wesley's discernment failed him. He could not make up his mind whether she was hysterical, artificial or genuinely inspired by the Spirit of God. In his indecision, Wesley relied upon the Gamaliel test: "If it be not of God, it will come to nought" (Acts 5:38. He should have gone on to finish the quotation, "If it is from God, you will not be able to stop these men; you will only find yourselves fighting against God.")

John Wesley can then assure us that if the Toronto blessing is not of God, it will fizzle out and come to nothing. If it is of God, nothing will stop it.

This article first appeared in
Healing and Wholeness April/May 1995
and we're grateful for permission to use it here.

Revival, Toronto and the Church Today
Maintaining Renewal in the Church
G. Howard Mellor
Principal, Cliff College

It is an enormous privilege for me to be here with you, to share in this day with Billy Abraham and to share with you thinking about revival and renewal. My task is to identify some of those factors which enable the sovereign work of God to be maintained in the life of the church. The subject is all the more pressing because there are some examples from church history that show how simple structures and strategy can strengthen and maintain the revival and renewal. Others tragically show that the absence of some inspired planning, or simple guidelines leads to the rapid evaporation of the divine work. It is true that Wesley seemed to do his planned in the wake of the spirit, but planning there was and it was inspired most of the time.

This rather leads us to question what revival is. J. Edwin Orr says he saw a sign in the San Fernando Valley that read, 'Revival every Monday.' Five miles down the road he saw another sign, 'Revival every night except Monday.' Given such a definition of revival, we can sympathise with a pastor who lamented, 'We had a long revival, but no one got revived!' (*Flames of Freedom* p 135).

One of the best definitions I know comes from the pen of Arthur Wallis, 'Revival is Divine intervention in the normal course of spiritual things. It is God revealing Himself to man in awesome holiness and irresistible power. It is such a manifest working of God that human personalities are overshadowed and human programmes abandoned. It is man retiring into the background because God has taken the field. It is the Lord .... working in extraordinary power on saint and sinner' (*In the Day of Thy Power* p.20). Lest look then at some things which are crucial in the church if revival and renewal are to be maintained.

Awe and intimacy

One of the intriguing things about the history of the last twenty years is the way that Charismatic Renewal took us through different types of spirituality. As a study of the Spring Harvest song books will show, that the early volumes carried many choruses which focused on a close personal relationship with God, for instance, 'When I feel the touch of your hand upon my life, it causes me to sing a song, that I love you Lord'. Many of the songs that were in those early song books began with 'I', (I will.., I want.., I'm gonna..)

More recent songs have focused on the holiness of Jesus; a God of awe and wonder. In my judgement, these songs have not had the impact of the earlier ones and have left many people in the evangelical and charismatic world with a very 'chummy' type of spirituality. A spirituality that is close, but not intimate. It is honouring to God but not standing in awe of God. One of the things that I see coming from the testimonies of those who have been to Toronto and those who have had close encounters with God, is that they develop the spirituality which is at one and the same time, both intimate with God and standing in awe of him. It is not surprising that this should be, for Paul to the Corinthians, describing the motives for mission says 'therefore, knowing the fear of the Lord we persuade men' (2 Cor 5:11), and three verses later indicates that 'the love of Christ controls us'(v14, which literally means propels us). The psalmists too, knew of this as Ps 23 and Ps 24 show.

All of this stems from a deepened awareness of God. Robert McCulloch says of the Cambuslang Revival, 'what was most remarkable was the spiritual glory of this solemnity; I mean the gracious and sensible presence of God.'

Such awe does not drive us to fear, though it may spur us on to holiness, rather it turns us to the very source of our being, it enables us to acknowledge the one from whom all good things come.

Such awe of the presence of God does not drive people away from him but curiously towards him. There is a magnetism to the awesome presence of God which enables us even to use the remarkably intimate word 'Abba' with him, to know and to feel him present.

> My God I Know, I feel thee mine,
> And will not quit my claim
> Till all I have is lost in thine
> And all renewed I am
> I hold thee with a trembling hand... (v2) HAP740

We need this sense of God in and with us as leaders of the church. How can we lead if first we have not been close enough to Jesus to be intimate, and yet also trembling at the awesome presence of God. God dealing with us as he wants to, which demands a real openness. We should remember here that pastors/leaders/evangelists are so good at hiding things.

Prayer in depth

> When praying with Jesus, we join his praying.
> Prayer is personal, it can be individual, but it is never alone
> because we pray with heavens host
> because there are millions around the world who also pray
> because we use the prayers of God's people down through the ages

John Wesley insisted 'when you seek God with fasting added to prayer, you cannot seek his face in vain.' (*Letters*, Vol V, p112) The Ulster revival of 1859 stemmed from a praying group of four young men at Kells. The Welsh outbreak in 1904 was kindled in prayer and Evan Roberts used to show people the worn mat in his room where he knelt to wrestle for the soul of Wales. An observer of the 1859 awakening in Wales indicated 'the great fruit of this revival is prayer. It was preceded by prayer, and it issues in prayer, which remains its chief agent ..... everyone is coming to believe in the efficacy of prayer.' (Evans, *When he is come: An account of the revival in Wales*, p59)

History belongs to the intercessors

in Rev 4-7 Jesus Christ, the lamb standing though slain is opening the seals. We come to the seventh seal (Rev 8:1-6). Heaven itself falls silent the heavenly host suspend their ceaseless singing so that the prayers of the saints on earth can be heard. The seven angels of destiny cannot blow the signal of the next times until the eighth angel gathers these prayers, they are mixed with the incense from the altar and rise silently before God. The angel takes the censor and hurls it at earth. Only then can the trumpets blow. A beautiful picture of human intervention in heavens liturgy. New alternatives are feasible, the people of earth have invoked heaven where all things are possible. In a real way history belongs to the intercessors. Not politicians or media spokespersons - but to those who pray.

Therefore let us call our people again to be and become the praying friends of Jesus crying out for the church and the world.

Wondering at his person love greatness life	- which we call	Adoration
Grateful for all He has done for us	- which we call	Thanksgiving
Being Ashamed	- which we call	Contrition/Penitence
With others on the heart	- which we call	Petition/Intercession
Renewal of commitment and friendship	- which we call	Dedication

We are   re-energised in Christs presence
        Cleansed by his purity
        Strengthened by his power
        Guided by his law
        Assured that He is with others and with us

What is vital for the church today is specific, prevailing prayer for without it a coming revival will not be as effective.

Holding fast to the truth

In the past revivals have also reflected a new and zealous regard for the scriptures. An awakening at Trevecca College in Wales in the winter of 1857 prompted this comment 'there was a beauty, a loveliness about the holy word which we had never hitherto perceived. New light seemed to be thrown upon it. It electrified us, and caused us to weep with joy. The feeling became general. All present were under its influence.' One of the things we should remember about the revivals in the 18th and 19th century was that the bible was in any case regarded as an authoritative document by the majority in society. That is very different for us today where our communities see the scriptures ridiculed and where pluralism has convinced people that it is merely one of a number of religious documents. If we are to show the same passion and commitment to the scriptures then it become absolutely vital that the scriptures are taught from the pulpit and that the people study the scriptures in groups and read them in their private devotions. There is widespread ignorance about the bible, especially the Old Testament. If a renewal is really going to sweep our communities then we need to begin opening up the scriptures to our people now.

That means a greater confidence in the scriptures that can be ours in a post-liberal world where the philosophy of the high modernity is being questioned, evangelical theology can rightly move to stage centre with renewed confidence.

Ministry and Counsel

George Hunter III, has in his excellent book *Reaching Secular People*, made it quite clear to us that people have all kinds of multiple hurts, alienated from society, alienated in their work, within their families and even within themselves. People view life as being out of control whether we are speaking about events of history, politics or their own personal lives.

These factors along with the rise of New Age and what I call soft occult, means there are many people who become Christians who have their lives entwined with influences that range from those who have dabbled in evil, those who are dangerously exposed, to the outright demonic; and such people require counsel and ministry. A parish minister, William McKnight, visited Cambuslang and talked with many who had been involved in the revival there. 'They .... discovered the gracious work of the Spirit of God upon their souls. In their confession of sin with shame, sorrow and blushing; in their professing a hatred of it, and loathing themselves on the account thereof, crying out behold we are vile we abhor ourselves and repent in dust and ashes.' (J Gillies, *Historical Collections*, (1845), p.1) George Whitfield describes a service under Thompson's ministry where 'arrows of conviction fled so thick and so fast, and such a universal weeping prevailed from one end of the congregation to the other, that good Mr Thompson could not help going from seat to seat, to encourage and comfort wounded souls.' (L. Tyerman, *The Life of George Whitfield*, Vol II, p79). Any who would be pastors and leaders today had better pray and work for skills in counsel and experience in prayer ministry for the wounded in our society.

Scriptural Holiness

One of the striking things about renewal and revival is that the new view of God, as mighty and holy has as impact on the lives of believers. I see it today in the people who have come to talk to me about their visit to Toronto. The same is true of earlier revivals. John Wesley reported about Kingswood Bristol that "The scene is already changed. Kingswood does not now as a year ago, resound with cursing and blasphemy. No more is it filled with drunkenness and uncleanness...it is no longer full of wars and fightings, of clamour and bitterness, of wrath and envying. Peace and love are there...(and in the evenings) they are at there usual diversion singing praise to God." (J Wesley, *Journal*, ed N. Curnock VolII, p322-3). McCulloch noted that the "drunken, tippling sot", was up at 3 or 4 in the morning in study of the Bible and prayer until 7 or 8. (A Fawcett, *The Cambuslang Revivals*, p39) Wives had a new affection for the husbands (and it is to hoped the husbands for their wives).

This Raises the question of why revivals should issue in such a changed life.

Rahtjen, Kramer and Mitchell talk about the nature of belief and how that affects our life in an interesting paper entitled *'Experiential Theology'*. In it they say that there are different forms of belief: Credal belief which is what we believe we believe (or feel we ought to), cerebral belief which is what we think we believe, verbal belief which is what we say we believe. BUT what we actually believe is what we do. Wesley had a lovely phrase to describe holiness, Love excluding Sin, by which he meant that the love of God is so fully present in the life of the Christian that there is no room for anything which is evil. This is extremely well presented by Arthur Skevington Wood in a paper called, *Love Excluding Sin*, which is contained in the new book about his life and work. (Taylor and Mellor, *Travelling Man*, Cliff College Publishing). Wesley knew that this teaching was key to the growth of Christians and the development of emerging Methodism.

Brings unity and dissension

It is of considerable interest to me that the Evangelical Alliance in the UK has felt it important to call a meeting for 19-20 December to do with the Toronto Blessing. Their hope for a time of 'openness and fellowship which will be profitable for evangelical unity.' They are trying to help people from different perspectives understand the history and theology of what is happening and at the same time to hear first hand what is taking place in various churches.

The idea of dissension is not new, whether caused by fear, envy, concern for orthodoxy. In Acts the then Faith and Order committee go to investigate the Samaritan mission and latter the Gentile mission. When William Grimshaw was involved in a revival at Haworth in 1742 the church though large was quickly full and many people remained outside. An extension was added, this remaining sufficient, with the converts being counted in dozens and hundreds. He was brought on a charge of preaching outside his own parish before Matthew Hutton, the Archbishop of York. He was asked 'how many communicants had you at your quarterly sacraments when you first came to Haworth?' 'Twelve my Lord.' 'How many have you now?' 'In the winter from four to five hundred, and sometimes in the summer nearly twelve hundred.' 'We cannot find fault with Mr Grimshaw decided the Archbishop as he is instrumental in bringing such numbers to the Lord's table'.

If we are in a revival time then there is no doubt that we shall see and even experience things which so far are beyond our experience and even imaginings. We need to challenge our fear, explain our concerns and broaden our vision. If that is true for us then it is also true for the church generally and we as leaders can have an impact there. In terms of the success and unity of a revival there is a lovely story about the Anglican Evangelical Revival in Truro in the mid 18th century.

It was said that St Mary's was so crowded that you might 'fire a cannon down every street of Truro in church time, without the chance of killing a single human being.' (E Sydney, *The Life and Ministry of Samuel Walker*, p 17). One of the things that seems to happen is a uniting of Christian people, a cessation of Christian hostility, and a lowering of denominational barriers. Long may it continue.

Revival and renewal can cause dissention because they are costly. The following quote puts the issues well. 'Revival and evangelism are not identical, although the word is frequently used to designate soul winning efforts directed toward unbelievers. Revival will always vitalize God's people .... but revival is not always welcome. For many its price is too high. There is no cheap grace in revival. It entails repudiation of self-satisfied complacency. Revival turns careless living into vital concern .... exchanges self-indulgence for self-denial. Yet, revival is not a miraculous visitation falling on an unprepared people like a bolt out of the blue. It comes when God's people earnestly want revival and are willing to pay the price' (*Christianity Today*, April 9, 1965).

Develop new fellowship structures

It has often been said that the genius of Wesley's work was that he started the Class Meetings. In every place I know where renewal of the church has had a long term affect, those who have been brought into the life of the church are also benefitting from a small fellowship/teaching/prayer group. Often based in a house. Indeed, some people come into the life of the local church through such a small group. Incidently, some observations that I have made in a number of churches is that people are far more likely to come by that route. What a remarkable error it has been for Methodist churches to loose this means of Grace.

Engage in the witness and work of God

Those who are recently converted and in whose heart and life the message of Christ is really stirred are much more likely to be bringing new people to Christ. In September 1833 the Presbyterian Synod of Ulster met for the purpose of mutual counsel and encouragement. In the introduction to the official report, the editor was able to write: 'The Lord in His inexpressible mercy has visited our Church with a season of abundant refreshment from His presence. In every direction there are evident signs of a revival. We bless God that He is raising up men of the true missionary spirit. Simple self-denying, energetic men, who seem to live for the gospel. The Synod of Ulster, we rejoice to say, are taking a prominent share in the heart-stirring operations of the present time. They have made a more decisive advance in spiritual life and power within the last few years than in the previous half-century.' Revival producing an unprecedented Zeal in evangelism - that is a recurring pattern in the story of the Church.

The 18th century zeal for evangelism created a huge missionary movement. In common with all previous revivals it united with a passion for justice and social action. The church as a result had an intensified desire to eradicate poverty and to work alongside the poor. The list of leaders who in the last century brought changes to the level of health, housing, education, prisons, care of children, the sick and the elderly becomes a list of leading of evangelicals. I fully expect the coming revival to have the same impact upon our society and to do more than that. In the past, Christians have sought to help the poor. Now it is also important to ask why are there poor people?

Physical expressions of God's presence

In *Power evangelism* and *Power Healing*, John Wimber noted these minor physical sensations that covered a wide range of physical effects in the presence of God. There has been the danger always that there is a focus on this rather on what God is doing. I call them minor recognising that some of them are quite dramatic, but nevertheless they are not the focus of what God is doing.

The following quote from John White is interesting. "..manifestations, while they may be a blessing, are no guarantee of anything. Their outcome depends on the mysterious traffic between God and our spirits. Your fall and your shaking may be a genuine expression of the power of the Spirit resting on you. But the Spirit may not benefit in the least if God does have his way with you, while someone who neither trembles nor falls may profit greatly." *When the Spirit Comes with Power* IVP 1987 p81-82

FALLING

There is common phenomena of people falling over in the meetings. The Vineyard Fellowships call it "resting in the Spirit" which is much better than the alternative "Slain in the Spirit". Such practice is not new nor should cause us alarm. People often retain a level of consciousness but are engaged with the Lord. Minister to them, pray over them. In my view do not just leave them.

The causes of falling in the bible vary from God putting people to sleep for a specific purpose; to falling out of holy fear, falling in prostration in the face of human arrogance and rebellion. The testimony of those falling today seems to enable divine intervention, rest and healing rather than contrition although there is some of that.

Key Bible texts : Gen 15:12, 1Sam 19, 2 Chron 5:13-14 (the text does not say they fell but that the glory (*kabod* which means weight) immobilized them, Ezek 1:28, Ezek 3:23, Dan 8:17, Dan 10:9, Matt 17:6, Matt 28:4, Jn 18:6, Acts 9:22 & 26, Acts 10:10, 2 Cor 12:1-4 (Paul describes a vision rather than a dream we are not told the physical position), Rev 1:17.

Historical notes: Jonathan Edwards, the main instrument and theologian of the Great Awakening in America (1725-1760), says in his *Account of the Revival of Religion in Northampton 1740-1742*:

> Many have had their religious affections raised far beyond what they had ever been before; and there were some instances of persons lying in a sort of trance, remaining perhaps for a whole twenty-four hours motionless, and with their senses locked up; but in the mean time under strong imaginations, as though they went to heaven and had there a vision of glorious and delightful objects.
>
> It was a very frequent thing to see outcries, faintings, convulsions, and such like, both with distress, and also admiration and joy.

It was not the manner here to hold meetings all night, nor was it common to continue them till very late in the night; but it was pretty often so, that there were some so affected, and their bodies so overcome, that they could not go home, but were obligated to stay all night where they were.

Charles Finney (1792-1875) was involved in one of the most powerful revivals. The following was noted about his ministry at a country place named Sodom, in the state of New York.

Finney gave one address in which he described the condition of Sodom before God destroyed it. 'I had not spoken in this strain more than a quarter of an hour' says he, 'when an awful solemnity seemed to settle upon them; the congregation began to fall from their seats in every direction, and cried for mercy. If I had a sword in each hand, I could not have cut them down as fast as the fell. Nearly the whole congregation were either on their knees or prostrate, I should think, in less than two minutes from the shock that fell upon them. Every one prayed who was able to speak at all.' Similar scenes were witnessed in many other places.

SHAKING

Shaking has been common at the meeting sometimes gentle and sometimes violent. The shaking come from a holy fear in the bible. The vineyard leaders seem to relate their experience more to prophetic ministry and impartation of spiritual gifts. My own observation is that people do shake for both reasons.

Key Bible verses : Dan 10:7, Ps 99:1 & 114:7, Jer 5:22, Jer 23:9, Hab 3:16, Acts 4:31, Jas 2:19

Historical notes: George Fox (1624-1691), founder of the Quakers: After a life-changing experience with the Holy Spirit, Fox had some remarkable experiences.

Fox was mightily used of God, and great conviction of sin fell upon the people to whom he preached. "The Lord's power began to shake them," says he, "and great meetings we began to have, and a mighty power and work of God there was amongst people, to the astonishment of both people and priests." Later, he says, "After this I went to Mansfield, where there was a great meeting of professors and people; here I was moved to pray; and the Lord's power was so great, that the house seemed to be shaken."

A remarkable power seemed to accompany the preaching of Fox wherever he went, whether in Britain or America, Germany, Holland, or the West Indies. He usually went about the country on foot, dressed in his famous suit of leather clothes, said to have been made by himself, and often sleeping out of doors or in some haystack. He was ridiculed and persecuted, beaten and stoned, arrested and imprisoned, more frequently perhaps than any other man, and yet the Lord seemed to greatly bless and own his labours. Describing his meetings at Ticknell, England he says: "the priest scoffed at us and called us 'Quakers.' But the Lord's power was so over them, and the word of life was declared in such authority and dread to them, that the priest began trembling himself, and one of the people said, 'Look how the priest trembles and shakes, he is turned Quaker also.'

DRUNKENNESS

There seem to be occasions when people have slurred speech, poor motor skills and giddiness which look to the casual observer like a person having taken too much drink. Is it this that Paul contrasts in Eph and suggests that spiritual filling is like being drunk with wine.

Key Bible verses: There are few texts, Jer 23:9, Acts 2:3, Eph 5:8. I am like a drunken man overcome by wine because of the Lord and his holy word. Jer 23:9.

CRYING

This is a common sign of the work of God. Weeping and repentance are often found together as Nehemiah's response makes clear (Neh 1). Observation over the last 20 years would have suggested that crying or weeping has become more regular in public worship and prayer meetings. I think I would have expected to find more incidents of weeping in the scriptures. In our Class meeting only this last week there was a time in the worship where many cried even to the point of wailing. Regularly this has been a feature of ministry in meetings.

Key Bible verses : 2 Chron 34:27, Neh 1, Ps 6, Jer 13:15-17, Luke 6:21.

Historical notes: On April 17, 1739, there was another remarkable case of conviction of sin, in Bristol. Wesley had just expounded Acts 4, on the power of the Holy Spirit, "We then called upon God to confirm his Word," says he. "Immediately one that stood by (to our no small surprise) cried out loud, with the utmost vehemence, even as the agonies of death. But we continued in prayer, till 'a new song was put in her mouth, a thanksgiving unto God.' Soon after, two other persons (well known in this place, as labouring to live in all good conscience towards all men) were seized with strong pain, and constrained to roar for the disquietness of their heart. These also found peace." Many other wonderful cases of conviction of sin attended Wesley's preaching. It was a frequent occurrence for people to cry aloud or fall down as if dead in the meetings, so great was their anguish of heart, caused, no doubt, by the Holy Spirit convicting them of sin.

LAUGHTER

The spontaneous eruption of laughter in the meeting.

Key Bible verses : Ps 126, Ecc 3:4, (Gen 17 Abraham and Sarah laugh, there are also references to joy eg Jn 17:13 which may include but does not necessitate laughter)

Historical Notes: Jonathan Edwards: It was very wonderful to see how person's affections were sometimes moved, when God did as it were suddenly open their eyes, and let into their minds a sense of the greatness of His grace, the fullness of Christ, and His readiness to save .... Their joyful surprise has caused their hearts as it were to leap, so that they have been ready to break forth into laughter, tears often at the same time issuing like a flood, and intermingling a loud weeping. Sometimes they have not been able to forebear crying out with a loud voice, expressing their great admiration. The manner of God's work on the soul, sometimes especially, is very mysterious.

PROPHETIC REVELATION

Key Bible verses : There many texts on this and far too many to quote here but this few give the flavour of the gift. Num 11:29, Num 11:6, 1 Sam 10:10, Acts 2:17-18 quoting Joel 2:28-32, 1 Cor 14. There seems little doubt that when the spirit of the Lord is at work among his people then there seems to be an increase in the amount of prophecy

Historical Notes: Dr F B Meyer, who visited the main centres of the Welsh revival, commented that no money was spent on advertising the meetings and that there was no need of posters on the hoardings. Lord Pontypridd likewise observed that the revival advertised and financed itself.

'There are no bills, no hired halls, no salaries,' he reported. The crowd flocked to the meetings simply to keep an appointment with God. More often than not they had no idea whether Evan Roberts or any other leader would be present or if they would speak.

Rodney 'Gipsy' Smith described an occasion at Maesteg where Roberts appeared after two and a half hours of prayer, praise an exhortation. 'Anybody would sing, even a little child. There was no speechmaking.' Roberts himself did not address the congregation. (J. E. Orr, *The Flaming Tongue*, p14-15).

The vineyard leaders have been trying to define the ways of coping with what is happening to them. They met in Oct 1994 and came up with the following guidelines for their leaders. They are working with the dilemma of being open but not permissive; giving guidance for running meetings without quenching the Spirit. They therefore suggest the following criteria:-
* Does it build up the community? Taking a lead form 1 Cor 14 the manifestations should be intelligible, edification is the primary criteria. If they are from God then they will build up, if from the devil then they will tear down.
* Does it exalt Christ? This is something they note from all the gifts in 1 Cor 12:3; 1 John 4:1-3; Rev 19:10.
* Does it resemble Christ's character? Only when the *charisma* is manifested as the expression of grace (humble selfless love) will it benefit either the individual or the community. (see J Dunn, *Jesus and the Spirit*)
* There will be unity and diversity in the community of Christ. Understanding is important. Order gives an etiquette to worship.

(A summary of the main findings of this meeting are to be found in *Alpha* magazine for December 1994.)

Who are used in revival?

It is simply not true that God uses anyone in revival. He tends to use those who are available to him, not necessarily those who are the greatest and the best. Ability is secondary to availability.

At the Kirk of Shotts in June 1630 the preacher was John Livingstone. He was only twenty-seven and not yet ordained. He shrank from the responsibility of delivering the extra sermon on the Monday following communion. He spent the whole night in prayer. By morning, we are told, 'there came such a misgiving of spirit upon him, on considering his own unworthiness and weakness, and the expectation of the people, that he was purposing to have stolen away, and declined the day's work.' In fact, he did actually leave the scene. Before he lost sight of the Kirk, however, some scriptural words conveyed a challenge from the Lord Himself: 'Was I every a barren wilderness or a land of darkness?' (cf Jer 2:31). That question was applied to Livingstone's heart with such overwhelming power that he was persuaded to return and fulfil his appointment to preach.

For no less than an hour and a half he had the utmost liberty in expounding Ezekiel 36: 25-26 - 'Then will I sprinkle clean water upon you, and ye shall be clean: from all your filthiness, and from all your idols, will I cleanse you. A new heart also will I give to you, and a new spirit will I put within you.' As a result, so we read, there was an unusual downpouring of the Holy Spirit, and more than five hundred of the hearers were affected, many of whom were themselves later employed as channels of revival. (J. Howie, *The Scots Worthies* p 316)

Few had heard of William McCulloch before the Cambuslang revivals of 1741 and 1742. His own son admitted that 'he was not a very ready speaker; though eminent for learning and piety, he was not eloquent .... His manner was slow and cautious, very different from that of popular orators.'

He was given the nickname of a 'yill' (or 'Ale') minister, for when he rose to speak, many of the audience would leave to quench their thirst in the public house. (Fawcett, p 39)

'The individuals who have been chiefly instrumental in the commencement and spread of the work .... have been men more distinguished for their piety, zeal, love of God, and compassion for souls, than for high attainments and intellectual powers .... The absence of great names, while at the same time a great and mighty spiritual work has been done, will the more effectually secure the glory to Him would alone giveth the increase.' (T. Phillips, *The Welsh Revival*, p 128).

<u>End Note</u>

In my judgement never has our society been so hedonistic; never so spiritually bereft; never so much in need of leadership; never so completely lost, as it is today. Our philosophy has sold out to secular existentialism, our media is sold out for sensationalism, our politicians have sold out to credit ratings, our manufacturing industry has just simply sold out. The protestant ethic is replaced by the national lottery, the faith of our fathers replaced by the influence of the New Age.

Never has there been such a time and never more need for God to move in a sovereign way to revive his church and rescue our society.

It seems to me that critics of revival and the movement of God want things to work through the existing structures. After all they say, everything should be done in a fitting and orderly way (1 Cor 4:40). The problem is that we each interpret this verse to mean that the Spirit of God will act in such a way as graciously to use the structures, the language and theology which we best know and understand. Things that are beyond the bounds of our ministry experience, actions that we take to be excesses, can all become a barrier in seeing that here God is at work.

It is of course true that we should recognise the tree by its fruit (Matt 12:33) and there is no doubt that the long term fruit of God (Gal 5:22) is the person and presence of Jesus Christ. The challenge to all of us today is this;

> That we take our faith and our hope and our courage in both hands,
> Yes and even our cynicism.
> That together we pray that God will keep us, the leaders of the church, at the point where we can recognise what he is doing;
> the humility to accept what he offers;
> the wisdom and insight to work with a God who ever overflows with goodness to renew the church.
>
> To Him be glory in the church now and for ever, Amen.